Turbulent Planet

Forest Furnace
Wildfires

Mary Colson

Raintree

www.raintreepublishers.co.uk
Visit our website to find out more information about **Raintree** books.

To order:
☎ Phone 44 (0) 1865 888113
📄 Send a fax to 44 (0) 1865 314091
💻 Visit the Raintree Bookshop at **www.raintreepublishers.co.uk** to browse our catalogue and order online.

First published in Great Britain by Raintree Publishers, Halley Court, Jordan Hill, Oxford OX2 8EJ, part of Harcourt Education Ltd. Raintree is a registered trademark of Harcourt Education Ltd.

Editorial: Charlotte Guillain and Isabel Thomas
Design: Michelle Lisseter and Bridge Creative Services Ltd
Picture Research: Maria Joannou and Virginia Stroud-Lewis
Production: Jonathan Smith
Printed and bound in China and Hong Kong by South China Printing Company

Originated by Dot Gradations
ISBN 1 844 43113 4
08 07 06 05 04
10 9 8 7 6 5 4 3 2 1

British Library Cataloguing in Publication Data
Colson, Mary
Forest furnace: wild fires. – (Turbulent planet)
1. Forest fires – Juvenile literature 2. Wildfires – Juvenile literature
634.9'618

A full catalogue record for this book is available from the British Library.

Photo acknowledgements
p.4/5, PA Photos/EPA; p.5 top, PA Photos/EPA; p.5 middle, Associated Press/Ric Francis; p.5 bottom, Corbis/Yves Forestier; p.6, Corbis; p.7, Popperfoto; p.8/9, Associated Press/Ric Francis; p.8, Rex Features/Ken James; p.9, Popperfoto; p.10, NASA/GSFC/LaRC/JPL, MISR Team; p.11, Reuters; p.12/13, FLPA/W. Meinderts/Foto Natura; p.12, FLPA/W. Meinderts/Foto Natura; p.13, Corbis/KJ Historical; p.14/15, OSF/Ronald Toms; p.14, Corbis/Patrick Bennett; p.15, NASA/GSFC/LaRC/JPL, MISR Team; p.16/17, Associated Press/Ric Francis; p.16, Trip/B. Vikander; p.17, Tudor Photography; p.18/19, PA Photos/EPA; p.18, Rex Features/Ken James; p.19, PA Photos/EPA; p.20/21, Popperfoto; p.20, Corbis/Raymond Gehman; p.21, Popperfoto; p.22, Image courtesy of Earth Sciences and Image Analysis Laboratory, NASA Johnson Space Center; p.22/23, Rex Features/Butler/Bruer; p.22, Rex Features/Butler/Bruer; p.23, Rex Features/Stewart Cook; p.24 left, Corbis/Nick Hawkes/Ecoscene; p.24 right, Corbis/Dan Lamont; p.25, Corbis/Yves Forestier; p.26/27, Spotfire Images/Mike McMillan; p.26, Associated Press; p.27, PA Photos/EPA; p.28/29, Corbis/Michael A. Yamashita; p.28, Corbis/Michael A. Yamashita; p.29, Corbis/Michael A. Yamashita; p.30/31, Science Photo Library/NASA; p.30, Photodisc; p.31, Corbis; p.32, Corbis/Paul A. Souders; p.33 bottom, Corbis/John Noble; p.33 top, Corbis/Jim McDonald; p.34/35, Rex Features/Sipa Press; p.34, Rex Features; p.35, FLPA/Derek Hall; p.36/37, PA Photos/EPA; p.36, Corbis/Raymond Gehman; p.38/39, Rex Features/Sipa Press; p.38, Popperfoto; p.40/41, Corbis; p.40, Associated Press/David Zalubowski; p.41, Getty Images/Stone; p.42, Still Pictures/Mark Edwards; p.43, FLPA/Fritz Polking

Cover photograph reproduced with permission of Topham Picturepoint

Contents

Any words appearing in the text in bold, **like this**, are explained in the glossary. You can also look out for them in the Wild words box at the bottom of each page.

Sparks

Fire legends

Ancient Greeks believed that Prometheus was the first person to bring fire to the Earth. He used a stick to collect fire from the Sun, where the gods had hidden it.

Native American Creek people told a story of how Rabbit swam to the island where the weasels were keeping fire. Rabbit set his own fur on fire and swam back to give fire to the people.

A forest fire can happen so quickly. Summer is fire season in lots of countries. When the weather is hot and dry, all it takes is the smallest flame to turn a healthy forest into a pile of ash. Within minutes, a fire can grow from a flicker to flames 50 metres high. The fire is hungry and there is a lot of dry forest to feed on. The wind helps the fire to spread quickly and easily. Animals run from their homes. Birds take flight to escape the heat, but not all are lucky. There is nothing to stop the forest **furnace**.

Fire facts

1 June

The fire season in the USA starts in June and ends in mid-October.

Every year worldwide, an area of forest three times the size of Wales is lost to burning.

Wild words   furnace   very hot fire
ranger   person who looks after a forest or national park

Smoked out

Rangers radio for help. They have been dreading this day. They struggle to fight back the flames and try to control this wild fire. **Smoke plumes** rise up from the treetops and thick blinding smoke fills the air. Trees explode as the heat boils away water and sap. The choking air makes breathing difficult, but rangers try to **stem** the flames as best they can. The wind swirls around, sending flames out in all directions. The rangers look out over the burning land. It is impossible to escape the melting heat. The forest fire is out of control...

Find out later...

How fast can a forest fire move?

Are all forest fires started by accident?

How can forest fires be stopped?

smoke plume   column of smoke
stem   check or stop

Mercury rising

The forest floor bakes under the summer sun. The earth cracks. Grasses and small plants dry out like straw. This happens in countries like the USA and Australia every summer. It also happens in tropical countries that have dry seasons. The places all over the world at risk from forest fires are shown in the map below.

Each season has a different temperature range. For example, summer is a lot hotter than winter. In summer or the dry season, the heat rises and there is less **humidity**. Humidity is the amount of **water vapour** in the air. There are two types of heat: wet and dry. When the sun has evaporated the water in the air, the heat is dry. The hotter and drier it gets, the greater the risk of fires.

Areas most at risk of forest fire tend to be very
▽ dry with little rainfall.

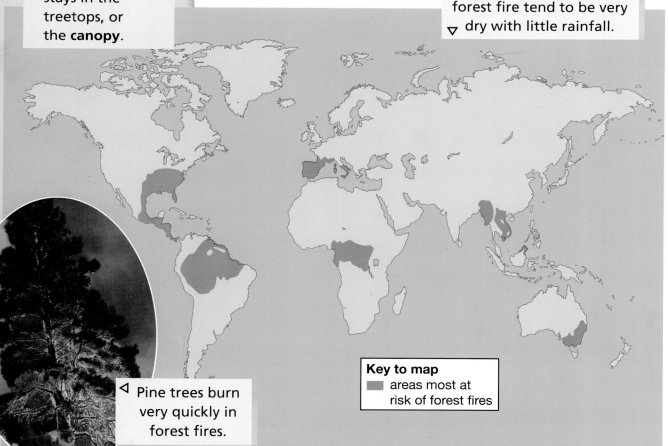

◁ Pine trees burn very quickly in forest fires.

Key to map
█ areas most at risk of forest fires

Wild words outback wilderness area in central Australia
vegetation plants

Bone dry

The forest floor is everything that is on the ground under the trees. This means all the plants that bind the soil together. Another word for this is **vegetation**. When the forest floor gets very dry, it can catch fire easily.

Fire whirl

Wildfires can produce hot winds that travel at up to 160 kilometres (100 miles) per hour. These winds are called **fire whirls**. They are a bit like tornadoes because the hot air spins around as it rises. They are very dangerous because they can hurl flaming logs and branches through the air. These burning objects start new fires wherever they land. These new fires are called **spot fires**.

Checkpoint

Forest fires – fires that are started naturally, by accident or on purpose in forests.

Wildfires – fires that burn out of control in the countryside, wilderness or **outback**.

Bushfires – uncontrolled fires in the outback or wilderness areas.

This forest fire in the Menai suburb of Sydney destroyed ▽ six homes in 1997.

water vapour   water in gas form
wildfire   out-of-control fire

Fast movers

Forest fires can move really fast. They can travel at
speeds of up to 23 kilometres (15 miles) per hour,
feeding on everything in their path. They can start new
smaller fires when the wind blows **embers** several
kilometres away. On a hot summer's day when **drought**
conditions are at their peak, something as small as a
spark from a train wheel can **ignite** a raging **wildfire**.

Fires spread because of fuel, weather and landscape. Fires
need dry vegetation such as leaves or wood for fuel. As the
fire moves, the heat dries out the fuel in front so that it is
ready to burn when the flames get there. If the weather
stays hot, the chance of wildfires gets higher and higher.

△ Firefighters risk their
lives to try and save
people's homes.

Wild words

drought   very dry weather, when it does not rain
ember   small piece of glowing coal or wood

Fire rages across Provence

In July 1999, more than 1000 fire-fighters battled a forest fire in Provence, France. Provence is a farming area dotted with pine forests. Special planes dropped water and foam on to the fire. But strong winds fanned the flames, making it harder to control them. Over 2400 hectares of forest were destroyed. Police suspected that the fire was started on purpose.

△ Rescuing family photos from a burning car is a risky business.

Hotspots

Hotspots are places around the world prone to forest fires. Hot countries like the USA, Australia and Indonesia have all suffered terrible damage as a result of fires.

Fire focus: China

Each year China struggles to contain wildfires. In 2002, over 5000 firefighters spent three weeks battling against an outbreak in the Hingghan Mountains. This area is home to half a million people. More than 200 square km (77 square miles) of forest were burned.

△ These firefighters in California, USA, are lighting a smaller fire to rob the main fire of fuel. They hope this will stop it from spreading further.

Fire focus: Indonesia

Tropical Indonesia in Southeast Asia suffers terrible wildfires. About half the country is rainforest, full of rare plants and animals. During the dry season, the rainforests become perfect fuel for forest fires.

Bushfire battle

Australia is an extremely dry country, which is why most of the population live near the coast. The middle of Australia is mainly made up of deserts and dry grasslands known as **bushland** or **outback**. Australia has many forests that cover about 6 per cent of the country. It has tropical rainforests in the north and large areas of dense forest and parkland in the south-west and south-east, particularly near Sydney, which is one of the major cities. Australia has long hot summers and mild winters, making fires a real **hazard**. Each state has a fire department that deals with **bushfires**.

In 2001, over 2500 square kilometres (950 square miles) of Australian bush were burned, killing thousands of sheep and destroying 150 homes. The estimated cost of the fire was Aus $18 million.

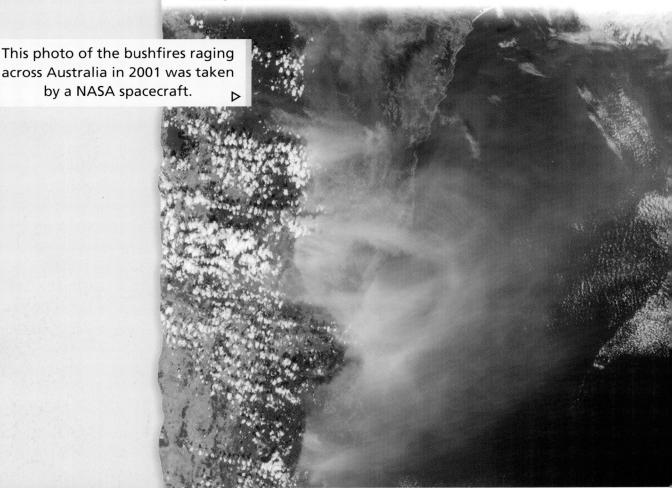

This photo of the bushfires raging across Australia in 2001 was taken by a NASA spacecraft. ▷

bushland   wild country in central Australia
hazard   danger

Wildfire woes

The USA has many forests and wilderness areas. The centre of the country is very hot and dry. In summer, **temperatures** can stay at 30 °C or above for weeks at a time. On average, 28,000 square kilometres (10,800 square miles) of forest land burn each year in the USA. This causes millions of dollars worth of damage, kills thousands of animals and brings misery to those who lose their homes.

To cope with the fires, there is a central office that works with firefighters, **rangers** and weather forecasters to **predict** blazes. In the USA in 2002, there were nearly 90,000 **wildfires** and around 70,000 square kilometres (27,000 square miles) of land burned. Colorado, Arizona and Oregon recorded their largest fires for a hundred years.

Fire facts

- In 2001–02, Indonesia suffered from raging forest fires.

- Smoke spread as far as Malaysia and southern Thailand, affecting 75 million people.

- Forty thousand people had to go to hospital with breathing problems.

- The fires cost an estimated US $6.5 billion in damage.

◁ In August 2003, a heatwave in Europe sparked huge forest fires in Portugal and Spain. Large areas of forest were destroyed and more than ten people died.

predict   to say when something will happen

Flashpoint!

On the alert

Rangers use radio and the Internet to check if there are fires in neighbouring areas.

The fire services, weather centre and air force all work together to spot the first sparks.

Although some fires start suddenly, there are warning signs that tell us a fire might break out. One of these is the **temperature**. Rangers keep a close eye on the **thermometer** in summer. When the temperature rises above 30 °C they sit up and take notice. For forest fires to start, the temperature needs to be high for a number of days. This is drying time for the **vegetation** on the forest floor.

Flashpoint

Everything has a temperature at which it will burst into flames: this is the **flashpoint** of a material. The flashpoint of wood is around 260 °C. At this temperature, wood releases a chemical that mixes with oxygen in the air and bursts into flames.

oxygen + heat + dry wood = wildfire!

△ Yosemite National Park often has forest fires. In 1996, a huge fire burned for almost a month.

flashpoint temperature at which something will burst into flames
heat transfer when fire dries out vegetation in advance

Burning up

To get a blaze under control, firefighters need to take away one of the factors that make a wildfire spread. They have to remove oxygen, heat or fuel.

Firefighters often try to steer the fire up a nearby hill. This is because of **heat transfer**. Heat from the fire rises up and dries out the vegetation further up the hill so it can also burn easily. The fire can then move quickly, drying and then burning. But once the flames reach the top, they slow down because heat transfer works slower going down. This means the firefighters have got a better chance of controlling the blaze on the hilltop. Fires often burn themselves out on hilltops because their dry fuel source has been used up.

△ Posters warn visitors to US parks to be responsible when travelling to areas at risk of fire.

△ Dry vegetation and scorching sunshine are perfect conditions for forest fires.

temperature   how hot or cold something is
thermometer   instrument used to measure temperature

On watch

Rangers are out and about all the time, checking for the first signs of fire trouble. They are the first line of detection and defence.

Out on the range

Across national parks and forestland in the USA, **rangers** keep watch in forest towers. These towers have equipment the ranger will need if a fire breaks out. Because towers can be quite **remote**, the ranger always carries a radio to call for help if needed. There are telephones and compasses in the towers too, so the ranger can describe the exact location of a fire to staff at base. Rangers in the towers also have binoculars so they can scan the landscape for signs of flames.

Rangers also **patrol** the land on foot and by helicopter, watching and waiting for the first sign of trouble. The rangers' work is vital to limit fire damage and protect houses near forestland.

Weather watch

More high-tech fire detective work is done at weather stations. Here, **meteorologists** can track weather patterns and forecast what the weather will be like over a period of days. They pass on this information to rangers who can plan, prepare and take action against the fire threat.

△ Rangers keep in contact with each other all the time in case a fire starts.

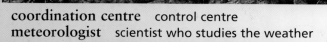

coordination centre   control centre
meteorologist   scientist who studies the weather

In the USA, there is a national forest fire weather **coordination centre** in Idaho. This is where all forest fires are reported and recorded. It is also where the most advanced weather forecasting takes place.

If a fire breaks out, rangers, firefighters and weather forecasters must keep in constant contact if they are to beat the blaze.

Heatwave hazards

Meteorologists use satellite **radar** pictures to predict where the next heatwave is coming from. This means they can warn the rangers, who can then try to prevent large forest fires starting.

△ This watch tower is located on Tenerife's Mount Teide.

△ Airborne dust, as shown in this photograph, can be an early sign of forest fire conditions.

radar   machine for spotting things at a distance
remote   a long way away

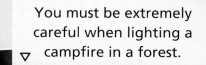

You must be extremely careful when lighting a campfire in a forest.

▽

Did you know...?

Most fires are caused by humans being **careless** and not thinking. Campfires and barbecues that are left burning cause over 80 per cent of all forest fires.

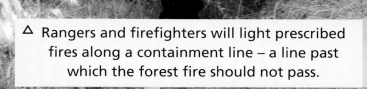

△ Rangers and firefighters will light prescribed fires along a containment line – a line past which the forest fire should not pass.

careless   not taking care
nutrients   chemicals that living things need to grow

Firestarter

Sometimes, **rangers** will come across a fire and decide to let it burn. Other times, they will deliberately start a fire. Strange as it seems, starting fires is exactly how rangers all over the world stop bigger fires breaking out. This is called **prescribed burning**. These small, controlled fires use up some of the dry fuel gathering on the forest floor. Animals can be herded elsewhere and people are told not to panic.

The rangers plan their prescribed burns carefully. They wait until the wind is low and the **temperature** drops. This way, they can control the flames and heat of their fire.

Why burn?

Prescribed burning has other benefits too. Fires clear the forest floor and make room for fresh young plants. New plants are rich with the **nutrients** released into the ground by the fire, and are good food for animals. Fires also kill pests like ticks and plant diseases. Clearing certain areas of land also makes it easier for humans and animals to live in and enjoy the forest. But rangers need to be careful. Terrible damage has been caused by prescribed burning that has gone wrong. The conditions have to be just right for it to be successful.

△ In New South Wales, Australia, a person can be fined Aus $5000 for dropping a cigarette on dry ground.

prescribed burning   where rangers start small fires for positive reasons
welding   using heat to join two pieces of metal

The big burn

> I filled the bath with water and cleared the gutters. **Hot ash embers** rained down on to my roof. A few streets away, a **fire whirl** ripped up 100-year-old trees and smashed them into houses.

A victim of forest fire.

What happens when fires burn out of control? If the weather stays hot and dry and the wind fans the flames, fires can sweep through whole regions in a matter of hours. Entire communities are reduced to a **smouldering** pile of **debris**. Crops are destroyed and animal homes eaten up along the way. Fires can jump roads and even jump streams. As long as the conditions are right, the fire will just keep on burning.

Feeding the flames

In December 2002, **bushfires** tore through New South Wales, Australia. Thousands of acres of forestland were destroyed as the Blue Mountains National Park went up in smoke. At the worst point, there were over 80 fires threatening the **suburbs** of Sydney.

evacuate   leave a place of danger
lava   red-hot liquid rock from a volcano

Bushfires threaten thousands

Wildfires continued to devastate the Blue Mountains National Park near Sydney yesterday. Firemen said they were losing the battle to control the fire. Helicopters dropped water bombs to stop the blaze but high winds today could make the situation much worse. Thousands of homeowners in the Sydney suburbs are preparing to **evacuate**.

The fire has already claimed two lives and at least nineteen homes have been destroyed. The sky over Sydney is thick with purple-black smoke. A local person said, 'I have not seen anything like it. Huge 100 metre flames just came down the hill like lava.' More than 4500 firefighters are continuing to battle against the blaze. Police suspect some of the fires have been started on purpose.

> " It looks like a **war zone.** "
>
> A **resident** describing a suburb destroyed by fire in Sydney, Australia.

Firefighters had to tackle this fire in three places across the city. ▽

△ Wildfire destroyed this suburb in Canberra, Australia. It was the worst natural disaster ever to hit the city.

> " It will stop either when there is **nothing left to burn** or it rains. "
>
> Fire Service spokesperson.

smouldering   burning slowly
suburbs   houses on the edge of a town or city

Fire focus: Florida, USA

From late May 2002, fires spread across the sunshine state of Florida. By the end of September, over 230 square kilometres (89 square miles) of forest and swamp had been burned. Two hundred homes went up in smoke. The **drought** was blamed for making the **vegetation** so dry. The air was full of smoke. Many people were short of breath and suffered from burning eyes, runny noses and coughs.

There was very little land left for animals to graze or live on. Water was **scarce** and many animals died. It was not just the fires that destroyed **habitats**, though. Bulldozers and diggers were used to create **firebreaks** and these also destroyed habitats. Luckily, most wildlife can escape and adapt to living in damaged areas.

> > > > > > > >

Turn to page 26 to find out about firebreaks.

Why 2002?

In 2002 over 70,000 fires burned nearly 30,000 square kilometres (11,560 square miles) of land in the USA. What made 2002 such a hot year? The record low global rainfall and **soaring** temperatures for much of the summer made perfect conditions for a blaze.

△ The singed fur of this elk calf is the result of a forest fire.

firebreak trench or strip of cleared ground to stop a fire spreading
habitat natural home of an animal

Fire focus: Colorado, USA

In the USA, Oregon and Arizona all reported record forest fire figures in 2002. But in the heavily-wooded state of Colorado, forest fires quickly became a daily nightmare.

This email was sent by Joe Nelson during the forest fires in Colorado, 2002.

From: Joe Nelson
Subject: Nightmare fires

The Missionary Ridge Fire is about 12 kilometres (8 miles) from my home. The sun is an orange spot in a smoke-filled sky. My children have been having problems with their eyes and lungs.

Wounded bears have been wandering into town and I have seen eagles and other birds die from the heat and smoke. I've watched them fall from the sky in mid-flight.

Food shortage

In countries where people depend upon their own harvest, forest fires can cause great human suffering. Many people in Indonesia suffered starvation after forest fires destroyed their crops in 2001. The government asked other countries to send food.

◁ Farmers help extinguish fires in an attempt to protect their crops.

scarce   hard to find
soaring   rising quickly

> The forest fire was several acres and **burning** very actively. I thought we were **goners**.
>
> Tom Albert, a former smokejumper.

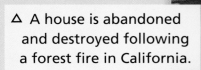

△ A house is abandoned and destroyed following a forest fire in California.

World news

In 2002 and 2003, **wildfires** were in the news all over the world. From North America to Australia, firefighters battled against furious flames.

In September, a wildfire raced through densely wooded mountains near Los Angeles, USA. Dozens of cabins were burned and thick clouds of ash and soot were spread across California.

After five days, the fire had already burned over 240 square kilometres (93 square miles) of the hot, dry foothills of the San Gabriel Mountains. The fire moved in three different directions, making it difficult for firefighters to contain.

More than 3000 firefighters battled the blaze. Thousands of **residents** were **evacuated**.

Turn to pages 28–29 to find out about smokejumpers.

evaporated   turned from water into water vapour
firestorm   very intense and destructive fire

Death as bushfires hit Canberra

Four people died and more than 400 houses were destroyed in the most severe fires to hit Australia for a decade. Canberra, the capital city of Australia, was surrounded by fires. A heat-wave and strong winds up to 85 kilometres (53 miles) per hour created a **firestorm** and drove the flames from the **outskirts** into the city. Changing winds and rising **temperatures** made it difficult to control the raging fires.

More than 2000 **residents** were evacuated and had to sleep in emergency shelters. A petrol station, a school and a fire station were all destroyed. Thousands of square kilometres of pine forests went up in smoke. One witness said, 'I lost count of the number of houses I saw on fire. One house literally exploded.' An 83-year-old woman was found dead on her lawn and a 61-year-old man died of smoke inhalation as he fought to save his house.

Smoke from wildfires covers the Los Angeles National Forest. ▽

Canada blazes

- In July 2002, forest fires broke out in Quebec, Canada.

- Huge clouds of thick smoke travelled across the border into the USA.

- The heat was so great that water dropped from planes **evaporated** before it hit the fires.

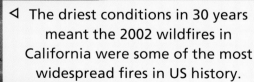

◁ The driest conditions in 30 years meant the 2002 wildfires in California were some of the most widespread fires in US history.

goner   person who is doomed
smokejumper   parachute firefighter for forest fires

Fighting the flames

Did you know...?
In the USA, if you are found guilty of starting a forest fire, you can be fined up to US $5000. In March 2003 a Forest Ranger was sentenced to 12 years in prison for starting Colorado's largest forest fire. In Australia, the maximum prison sentence for starting a wildfire is 25 years.

There are many people working to protect the public from the dangers of forest fires. There are ground and air emergency services on call to combat the flames. In some countries, there are even special air divisions of firefighters who travel around providing assistance. And of course, there are the firefighters on the ground who battle against the mighty flames all the time.

Cross-country

Managing fire control is very difficult, especially in large countries. In the USA, there are eleven **coordination centres** that organize the planes and people to go and fight the fires. In some countries, special fire engines are used for fighting **wildfires**. These engines are heavy-duty, **off-road** vehicles with a small crew. They can carry up to 3600 litres of water.

▽ Even burning garden waste in dry areas can lead to a fine of Aus $10,000.

Waterbombers

Once a forest fire gets underway, it needs to be tackled from the ground and the sky. Special planes and helicopters carry huge amounts of water over the fires and drop it on the flames. These amazing aircraft are called **airtankers** or 'waterbombers'. Some can drop 136,000 litres of water in an hour.

The helicopters can refuel from any water source, ranging from a stream or a tank on a lorry to the ocean. As long as the water is at least 45 centimetres deep, they can fill their massive water tanks in minutes. The helicopters carry huge slings underneath that can scoop up water from a pond or a lake. These 'Super Scoops' can carry around 12,000 litres. That is over 24,000 soft drink cans!

Fire fact

Waterbombers drop **fire-quenching** chemicals in a line. This slows the fire down in order to give firefighters on the ground time to build a **firebreak**. Pink dye is added so the pilot can see where the line is.

This airtanker is dropping water over a forest fire in the south of France. ▷

fire-quenching   able to put out fires
off-road   designed for rough stretches of land

In the line of fire

One of the best ways to fight forest fires is to dig a **firebreak**. This is a gap that the fire cannot cross. If possible, firefighters use streams, roads or open spaces to make the firebreak. If not, a firebreak has to be dug. Firefighters use axes, shovels and even bulldozers to clear away all the brush, logs and forest **debris**. This break is usually about 10 metres across. It has to be wide enough to prevent the fire leaping across it. The edges of the firebreak are then soaked with water or chemicals to slow the burning.

Only when the firebreak is ready will the firefighters light the **backfire**.

Backfire

The backfire is lit to burn the area between the firebreak and the forest fire itself. The idea is that the fire that the firefighters have lit will burn up any spare fuel and meet the oncoming fire. With nothing for it to feed on, the main fire will burn itself out. A backfire is one way firefighters can take away fuel from a fire. It is very dangerous and risky but with luck, the two fires will meet and burn each other out.

Flameproof

All forest firefighters in the USA carry a flameproof tent that provides shelter away from the flames. Fire shelters can be put up in 20 seconds. The firefighter lies on the ground inside as the fire rages on overhead. It is safer on the forest floor as it is the coolest place.

Areas 'at risk' from fire will be **evacuated** immediately. ▽

backfire   fire that is lit to burn up the fuel that is feeding the main fire
Hotshot   specialist firefighter for forest fires

Hotshots

In the USA, some of the most **specialized** firefighting teams are called 'Hotshots'. These highly-trained, skilled crews are made up of firefighters who have had at least one season's experience as a wildland firefighter. Hotshots are sent to the most dangerous part of a fire.

Firefighters must act quickly if they are to minimize damage from forest fires. ▽

Checklist

Forest firefighters need a lot of equipment:

- ✓ Helmet
- ✓ Boots
- ✓ Torch
- ✓ Pulaski – a cross between an axe and a pickaxe
- ✓ Combined rakes and hoes
- ✓ Shovels
- ✓ Chainsaws
- ✓ Explosives
- ✓ Special cooling spray

Fire-resistant rucksacks help forest firefighters carry special equipment. ▽

specialized expert

Smokejumpers

Smokejumpers are amazing people. They throw themselves out of aeroplanes over blazing forest fires. Smokejumpers are airborne firefighters. Using parachutes and wearing helmets and heat suits, they drop into the trees. All their equipment has to be sent down with them. They work in very small teams to create a **firebreak**.

When the alarm is raised, smokejumpers are sent to **remote** fires in wilderness areas because they can get there in a hurry. Equipment is dropped in separate parachutes. When the fire is out, the smokejumpers often have to pack up and get out, carrying more than 45 kilograms of equipment each.

How it all started

The United States Air Force and the Forest Service thought it would be a good idea to have an early warning system for forest fires. In 1925 they teamed up and planes started **patrolling** the skies over forests during the summer months. The pilots had a bird's-eye view of the forest below and they could spot any smoke or flames and tell the **rangers**.

Fire Fact

Smoke jumping, an idea first developed in the 1920s, allows firefighters to tackle fires from remote locations.

◁ A smokejumper waits on a runway with all his equipment.

Wild words   clearing   small space in a forest or wood
patrolling   going round at regular times to check something

Smokejumpers preparing to jump into a blazing fire. ▷

Fire facts

- Smokejumpers are taught to sew so they can repair their own parachutes.

- Smokejumper Dale Longanecker holds the jump record of over 600 jumps.

- Over 400 smokejumpers cover the USA and Canada.

In the early days, it was thought that dropping firefighters into burning **wildfires** by parachute would be too risky. Eventually, people came round to the idea and lots of test drops were done to see what sort of problems the jumpers might meet. Special parachutes, equipment andclothing were designed. The very first jumpers went into action on 12 July 1940.

◁ You must have at least one year's experience of fighting forest fires on the ground before you can apply to become a smokejumper.

Smoke and ashes

Satellite patrol

High above the Earth, an unmanned satellite called *Terra* (meaning 'earth') monitors all the forest fires burning around the globe. Scientists on the Earth can then study how forest fires affect weather. In 2002, *Terra* mapped severe fires everywhere from the Americas to Australia.

When trees burn, they release carbon dioxide gas. In large quantities, this gas upsets the balance of gases in the Earth's atmosphere. When vast areas of forest burn, a lot of carbon dioxide is released into the air that we breathe.

Scientists believe that smoke from the Indonesian fires in 1997 has added to the **greenhouse effect**. This is the main cause of **global warming**. In 1997, the amount of harmful carbon dioxide released into the air was higher than normal. During this time, thousands of square kilometres of Indonesia's national forests were destroyed. Some of the fires were caused by farmers clearing forestland to plant crops. These deliberate fires have caused many problems around the world.

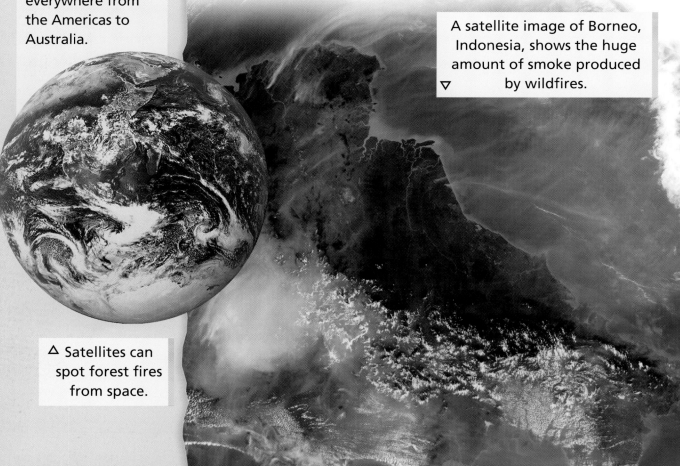

A satellite image of Borneo, Indonesia, shows the huge amount of smoke produced by wildfires. ▽

△ Satellites can spot forest fires from space.

clutch   hold tightly
greenhouse effect   trapping of heat by certain gases in the atmosphere

Gasping for breath: the killer smog

Indonesia, September 1997. Terrible forest fires continue to burn as smoke blows across Indonesia. Firefighters are helpless in the face of such enormous and widespread burning.

Huge areas of the country are suffocating under awful yellow **smog**. Many towns and cities have been almost swallowed by this smog. It is often hard to see beyond 100 metres. Cars are using headlights in the middle of the day.

People move like ghosts in and out of the smog. They **clutch** their shirtsleeves to their faces to protect themselves. Schools and businesses are closed in neighbouring countries like Malaysia, and people have been advised to stay indoors as much as possible. Millions across the region are gasping for breath.

Measuring air

- The Air **Pollutant** Index measures how much pollution is in Asian air. A score of more than 100 means that the air is unhealthy.

- After the 1997 fires in Indonesia, some areas had scores of 839.

△ During the fires of 1997, many Indonesians wore face masks to protect them from harmful smog.

pollutant harmful substances in the air, water or on land
smog fog or haze caused by smoke or pollution

Amazing Amazon

Some parts of the world have huge forests called rainforests. Rainforests are vital for human life because they produce oxygen for us to breathe. Without these forests, humans would die. The Amazon rainforest in Brazil is the most famous in the world, but it is under threat.

Deforestation

Deforestation is when forest is removed, burned or destroyed. Once the trees and bushes are no longer there, the soil becomes very dry and erodes easily. In places like Brazil, the USA and Indonesia, farmers are deliberately destroying forests and rainforests by clearing the land for farming and by **logging**.

It is estimated that 15 per cent of the Brazilian Amazon rainforest has disappeared over the last 30 years. That is an area the size of France.

Will luscious rainforest landscapes like this be a thing of the past one day? ▽

These photographs show forest in Tasmania, Australia, before and after fire struck. ▷

barren   infertile
deforestation   when forest is removed, burned or destroyed

Ecological effects

Deforestation changes the surface of the planet very quickly. Where trees once stood, there will be **barren** soil. Not only does the smoke from the fires threaten human health, but forest fires also destroy animal **habitats** and **grazing land**. Tropical rainforests also have many rare plants that may hold the cures for diseases. Once they are gone, they are lost forever.

Forest fires started on purpose can quickly rage out of control.

Fire facts

- In 2002, smoke from forest fires delayed flights at two airports in Moscow, Russia.

- Each year in Europe, forest fires destroy around 7800 square kilometres (3000 square miles) of land. The cost per square kilometre is between £70,000 and £350,000.

grazing land   fields of grass for animals to eat
logging   cutting down trees and selling the wood

Landslide!

The damaging effects of forest, bush and **wildfires** are not over once the fire has been put out. The dry, scorched earth may crack and split. If heavy rains fall after a fire, the water makes the soil **unstable**. The land is too dry to absorb water, so landslides and mud rivers are common.

Rivers of mud

In July 1994, tonnes of mud and rock poured on to a 5-kilometre (3-mile) stretch of motorway on Storm King Mountain, Colorado, USA. Thirty cars were washed away and two were swept into the Colorado River.

2002 was a long hot summer in Southern China. After the forest fires, the earth was cracked and dry. Torrential rains came and caused landslides in hilly areas. More than 1000 people were killed.

△ Firefighters are trained to use all kinds of equipment including chainsaws.

Fire facts

- The annual cost of forest fires around the world runs into the billions.

- In 2002, 4000 square kilometres (1500 square miles) of land were burned in Colorado and Oregon in the USA.

△ An area destroyed by forest fire could also face landslides and flooding.

charred   blackened by burning
flammable   easily set on fire

Renewed earth

Forest fires can cause a lot of damage but they can also change some things for the better. Fire clears away old growth in forests and makes the **charred** plants release **nutrients** into the soil. This makes the ground more fertile so new plants can grow easily.

Renewed by fire

Savannah is grassland dotted with a few trees and bushes. East Africa has a lot of areas of savannah. They are very dry places that are hit by fires every year. The grasses survive the flames because their stems lie just beneath the ground. So although the leaves are burnt, the plants will sprout new shoots when the rain comes.

Australian Mountain Ash trees also benefit from fires. They are one of the tallest trees in the world, growing over 90 metres high. As fire burns the forest around them it chars their trunks, but cannot reach the leaves at the top. After the fire has passed, mountain ash seeds fall to the bare ground. They can then grow quickly, without any other plants nearby to compete for nutrients.

Burning bark

- Some trees shed their bark when they burn and release **flammable** oils from their leaves, making the fires worse.

- Other trees, like the Mountain Ash in Australia, actually need a forest fire to clear the land before they can grow.

△ The Australian Grass Tree flowers after wildfires.

unstable   likely to move or change

Be prepared

Smokey Bear

In the USA, Smokey Bear has been teaching children about forest fire safety for 50 years. His motto is 'Only you can prevent wildfires'. Smokey gives tips on fire safety on television, in schools and on a special website.

All over the world people love to get out and enjoy the great outdoors. But fires are such a danger in the summer months that great care needs to be taken.

In both Australia and the USA, there are lots of organizations giving advice. Here are some top tips for safe campfires.

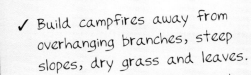

✓ Build campfires away from overhanging branches, steep slopes, dry grass and leaves.

✓ Clear campfire site down to bare soil and circle the pit with rocks.

✓ Keep a bucket of water and a shovel nearby.

✓ Never leave a campfire unattended.

✓ Never play with matches, lighters, **flammable** liquids, or any fire.

✓ Tell your friends about fire prevention.

△ Smokey Bear watches as a forest ranger teaches a child how to put out fires.

lunar landscape   like the surface of the Moon
predator   animal that hunts other animals

Caught by the flames

If someone is trapped by flames, firefighters are quick to organize themselves. They make a base in a safe area nearby and get going. It is a constant battle to control fires. Fire teams have to work quickly to protect people and property. Here is a description from a lucky survivor of the 2002 fires in Arizona, USA.

From: Matthew Francis, Arizona
Subject: Arizona Fires 2002

The high school where I went is now a staging area for men with pickaxes, walkie-talkies and fire-resistant clothing.

The bulldozers have turned what was our garden into a **lunar landscape** in an effort to starve the fire.

Tonight, the blaze is still creeping, like a **predator** lying in wait.

66

The fire **trapped** us in the house. We couldn't get out. You know you are going to **die** if you stay in.

99

Sandra Johansen, Australia.

◁ US Forest Service Firefighters work to control a fire thought to be started by an illegal campfire.

High alert

All around the world, government officials warn people of the dangers of forest fires. From Australia to Europe and America to Southeast Asia, the same warnings are given. But the results depend on what resources are available.

In March and April 2002, forest fires raged in Vietnam. The hot dry seasons of the previous few years meant that forests were very dry. Fires destroyed almost half of a forest reserve that was home to rare animal and plant species. Vietnam does not have enough resources to fight major fires. Fire-fighting helicopters would have saved many hectares of forest, but the government does not have the money even to buy fuel for the flights.

This girl lost her home in a fire that left 658 families homeless in Borneo, Malaysia. ▽

Domestic defence

In high-risk areas, builders use fire-resistant materials when building new houses. This means materials that will not burn. Houses in places like Sydney, Australia are mostly made of brick. This should protect them from the worst of a **wildfire**.

△ It is vital that people understand the dangers of forest fires – maybe scenes like this will then become a thing of the past.

Along with tourism, wood and paper production are important parts of Vietnam's economy. If the forests go up in flames again, many aspects of life and business will suffer. Around 20,000 people depend on the forests for gathering wood and hunting for food.

Wales, UK, 2003

Fires rage in forests and moors

More than 100 firefighters are battling a forest blaze that is being spread by strong winds. A helicopter dumped water-bombs from the sky while dozens of houses and a children's home were **evacuated**. Senior Police Officer Gareth Pugh said, 'It is an enormous fire and it has done environmental damage already'. The fires are destroying trees and moorland, which were left dry by an unusually hot spring. Fire crews are hoping for rain to help them fight the fire.

△ Sometimes, forest fires take communities by surprise. In spring 2003, the UK suffered fires in Scotland and Wales.

The Home Guard

When a fire is burning in Australia, people protect their homes by pouring water into gutters and damping down wooden fences around their property. Most people in country areas have a water tank and some have **generators** and pumps so they can become firefighters themselves.

A flaming future?

Did you know...?

Every year, diseases and pests destroy nearly seven times more forest than fires do.

People are working hard to cope with the problem of forest fires and **wildfires**. Environmental agencies study why fires get out of control. In countries like Brazil, farmers are given money to stop them burning the forests. Governments are also educating people.

In Cape Town, South Africa, forest fires have closed highways because of the thick black smoke they produce. South Africa has long hot summers and the forest floors become very dry and easily **ignited**. Radio, television and the Internet are very important here in warning people about dangerous fires. People can track the fires and get ready to **evacuate** the area if necessary.

△ Fires are not to blame for all the deforestation that takes place on the Earth.

global warming   rise in the temperature at the Earth's surface due to an increase in the greenhouse effect

Global change

Forests need protecting and looking after. They are vital for life on Earth because they create oxygen for humans to breathe. Plants in the forests may provide science with cures for many diseases.

In 1992, in Rio de Janeiro, Brazil, there was an important meeting between the leaders of many countries from all over the world. This meeting was known as the Earth Summit. Its purpose was to look at ways to help stop **global warming**. The leaders agreed to work together to protect forests from being cut down or burned for land clearance. Some progress has been made but there is still a long, long way to go.

△ Horses flee as fierce fire threatens their **habitat**.

Did you know...?
A water-carrying airship is being designed to carry and drop 1,200,000 litres of water over forest fires. That is the same amount of water carried by 1000 helitanker lifts.

△ Helicopters are used in many parts of the world to help extinguish fires.

Burnout?

Although forest fires are dangerous and can claim lives, they are a very important natural process. Organizations around the world work together to share information about the positive and negative aspects of forest fires. The United Nations has an Environmental Programme that gathers information from different countries and gives advice on how to manage the flames. Forest fires can threaten the safety of humans and animals. But they are also a way of killing off diseases and pests. One thing is certain: forest fires will continue to happen and continue to renew the soil, whatever the cost.

Fire fact

After a time, burned and cleared forest floor can be used as fertile farmland. In many parts of the world, people take advantage of the good soil to grow their own food.

Many families are moving away △ from overcrowded cities in Indonesia to build homes and farms in cleared rainforests.

burnout   when a fire has burned itself out
ecosystem   relationship between animals and their environment

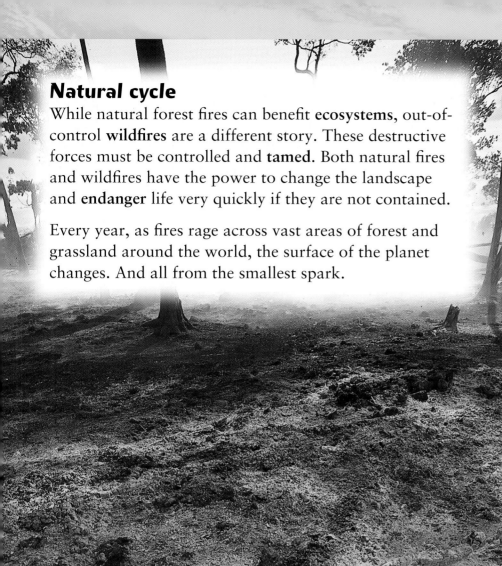

Natural cycle

While natural forest fires can benefit **ecosystems**, out-of-control **wildfires** are a different story. These destructive forces must be controlled and **tamed**. Both natural fires and wildfires have the power to change the landscape and **endanger** life very quickly if they are not contained.

Every year, as fires rage across vast areas of forest and grassland around the world, the surface of the planet changes. And all from the smallest spark.

> The whole sky went **dark grey**, as if a **massive storm** was **brewing**.

A resident of New South Wales, Australia, describing a fire near his home.

◁ Recently burned forests will soon provide ideal growing conditions for new plants.

endanger   to put something or someone at risk of being harmed
tamed   brought under control

Find out more

Organizations

Smokey Bear

US organization with fire safety information and advice for adults and children. The website features games and quizzes.

smokeybear.com

National Interagency Fire Centre

This website has great maps showing where fires occur around the world.

wildfirenews.com

BBC Science

News, features and activities on all aspects of science and natural disasters.

bbc.co.uk/science

New South Wales National Parks

Information on fire prevention and control in Australia.

npsw.nsw.gov.au/parks

Books

Awesome Forces of Nature: Blazing Bush and Forest Fires
   L. and R. Spilsbury (Heinemann Library, 2003)
Green Fires: Wildlife in Danger
   Steve Parker (Heinemann Library, 2003)
Nature on the Rampage: Fires
   Tami Deedrick (Raintree, 2003)

World Wide Web

If you want to find out more about forest fires, you can search the Internet using keywords like these:

- wildfire + news + [date you are interested in]
- 'acid rain' + landslide
- deforestation + fire
- fires + 'global warming'
- forest fires + KS3

You can also find your own keywords by using headings or words from this book. Use the search tips on page 45 to help you find the most useful websites.

Search tips

There are billions of pages on the Internet, so it can be difficult to find exactly what you are looking for. For example, if you just type in 'fire' on a search engine like Google, you will get a list of 32 million web pages. These search skills will help you find useful websites more quickly:

- Know exactly what you want to find out about first
- Use simple keywords instead of whole sentences
- Use two to six keywords in a search, putting the most important words first
- Be precise – only use names of people, places or things
- If you want to find words that go together, put quote marks around them, for example 'smoke jumper' or 'heat transfer'
- Use the advanced section of your search engine
- Use the + sign to add certain words, for example typing + KS3 into the search box will help you find web pages at the right level.

Where to search

Search engine

A search engine looks through the entire web and lists all the sites that match the words in the search box. They can give thousands of links, but the best matches are at the top of the list, on the first page. Try **bbc.co.uk/search**

Search directory

A search directory is more like a library of websites that have been sorted by a person instead of a computer. You can search by keyword or subject and browse through the different sites in the same way you would look through books on a library shelf. A good example is **yahooligans.com**

Glossary

airtankers   water-carrying planes

backfire   fire that is lit to burn up the fuel that is feeding the main fire

barren   infertile

burnout   when a fire has burned itself out

bushfire   uncontrolled fire in the bush or outback

bushland   wild country in central Australia

canopy   top of a forest, the treetops

careless   not taking care

charred   blackened by burning

clearing   small space in a forest or wood

clutch   hold tightly

coordination centre   control centre

debris   rubbish

deforestation   when forest is removed, burned or destroyed

drought   very dry weather, when it does not rain

ecosystem   relationship between animals and their environment

ember   small piece of glowing coal or wood

endanger   put something or someone at risk of being harmed

environment   the world around us

evacuate   leave a place quickly to avoid danger

evaporated   turned from water into vapour

firebreak   trench or strip of cleared ground to stop a fire spreading

firestorm   very intense and destructive fire

fire-quenching   able to put out fires

fire whirl   whirlwind created by the heat from a forest fire

flammable   easily set on fire

flashpoint   temperature at which something will burst into flames

furnace   very hot fire

generator   machine for producing electricity

global warming   rise in the temperature at the Earth's surface due to an increase in the greenhouse effect

goner   person who is doomed

grazing land   fields of grass for animals to eat

greenhouse effect   trapping of heat by gases in the atmosphere

habitat   natural home of an animal

hazard   danger

heat transfer   when fire dries out vegetation in advance

Hotshot   specialist firefighter for forest fires

humidity   wetness in the air

ignite   start a fire

lava   red-hot liquid rock from a volcano

logging   cutting down trees and selling the wood

lunar landscape   like the surface of the Moon

meteorologist   scientist who studies the weather

nutrients   chemicals that living things need to grow

off-road   designed for rough stretches of land

outback wilderness area in central Australia

outskirts edge of a city or town

patrolling going round at regular intervals to check something

pollutant harmful substance in the air, water or on land

predator animal that hunts other animals

predict say when something will happen

prescribed burning where rangers deliberately start small fires to prevent larger ones

radar machine for spotting things at a distance

ranger person who looks after a forest or national park

remote a long way away

resident person who lives in the area

scarce hard to find

smog fog or haze caused by smoke or pollution

smokejumper parachute firefighter for forest fires

smoke plume column of smoke

smouldering burning slowly

soaring rising quickly

specialized expert

spot fire small outbreak of fire

stem check or stop

suburbs houses on the edge of a town or a city

tamed brought under control

temperature how hot or cold something is

thermometer instrument used to measure temperature

unstable likely to move or change

vegetation plants

water vapour water in gas form

welding using heat to join pieces of metal

wildfire out-of-control fire

Index

Raintree freestyle Curriculum version

Series in the *Freestyle Curriculum Strand* include:

Turbulent Planet

Energy Essentials

Incredible Creatures

Material Matters

Find out about the other titles in these series on our website www.raintreepublishers.co.uk